Laudate pueri Dominum
laudate Nomen Domini

The Holy Infant
of Prague

Dedicated
to all worshippers
of the Prague Infant Jesus,
whether
they are living
or dead

Laudate pueri Dominum
Laudate Nomen Domini Pau

Sanctum Nomen ejus *Luc. 49.*

Translated by
Norah Hronková

ISBN 80-85955-97-0

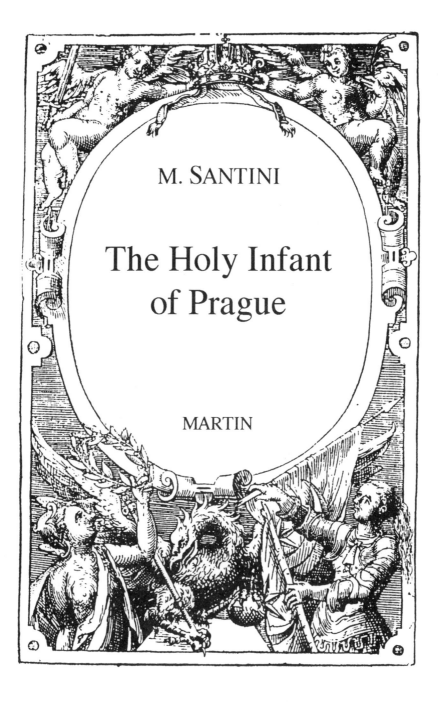

M. SANTINI

The Holy Infant
of Prague

MARTIN

In Lieu of an Introduction

In the heart of Europe there lies the country of the Czech nation, Bohemia.

In the heart of Bohemia there is the capital city of the ancient Bohemian kingdom, Prague.

And in the heart of Prague there stands an age-old church.

Let us visit this place, one of the most notable in the whole country.

For more than three hundred and fifty years this church in the heart of Europe, in the heart of the Bohemian land, has been the home of one of the most famous miracle statues – the home of the Prague Child Jesus.

Prayers from all over the world fly ceaselessly to this holy place. At this very moment innumerable hands are clasped in prayer all over the world, innumerable lips whisper their wishes, innumerable believing souls breathe out their supplications.

It has been said that the Lord of the universe has chosen places where he proves his might and places where he shows his mercy. And the Lord of the universe's love of man flows from the merciful Prague Child Jesus.

Let us visit this "little Prague dweller" as the Prague Child Jesus is called. This booklet invites you to take part in the eventful story of the most famous destination of pilgrimages in the Czech Lands.

The doors of the ancient Carmelite church are opening...

The Prague Child Jesus is awaiting us, as he awaited our forefathers. He is prepared to help us, as centuries ago he helped our ancestors.

In the dusk of the age-old church a glow spreads out from the divine child, sending its rays into the most distant corners of the earth from which prayers come...

May the words of the old song glorifying the Prague Child Jesus be fulfilled today, as they have been through the centuries:

You as Prague's precious gem do shine
The gateway to bliss so pure
Pour joy into our hearts that pine
Of comfort we can be sure!

THE LEGEND OF THE ORIGIN
OF THE PRAGUE CHILD JESUS

legend emerges from the dusk of the ages. It comes to us as it has come to believers down the centuries. Let us listen to it. For not even scientific works dealing with the Prague Child Jesus know its origin exactly – they indicate that it is wreathed in mystery.

And it is just from the darkness of mystery that the voice of ancient legends sound...

Long, long ago the Christians waged fierce battles with the heathen on the Pyrenean peninsula. In those days an ancient monastery stood not far from Seville.

Its church and monks' cells were pervaded with prayer, the monastery gardens were pervaded with the plashing of fountains and the scent of flowers. But it happened that an enemy army advanced on the monastery.

The Moores conquered the monastery and destroyed it.

After a time four monks who had survived the destruction of their monastery returned to that devastated place and settled into the ruins. They endeavoured to return the monastery to its former beauty, spending their days in work and in prayer.

Yet though the monks worked hard the monastery rose from the ruins very slowly.

Then it happened that a blue sky was glowing over the monastery on one of those glorius summer days that make one want to sing.

And a little child came up to one of the monks who was working in the monastery garden and invited him to pray.

Why should I not pray, thought the monk. Indeed I should pray from morning to evening to give thanks for having survived the destruction of my monastery. And I should pray especially today, as I have been allowed to live to see such a beautiful day.

He clasped his hands, knelt down in the sweet-smelling, flowering garden and started to say the angelic greeting.

He prayed and he felt an immense gratitude...

"...the blessed fruit of your life, Jesus," he finished and raised his eyes, filled with tears of gratitude, to look at the child.

"I am Jesus," said the child and smiled at him.

The monk gazed at the child in astonishment. He strove to engrave the features of this strange visitor on his memory as firmly as he could. But the child... was gone. It had disappeared. The burning air quivered where it had appeared a moment before.

Years passed.

The monastery was now filled with new monks. The broken walls had been re-erected, new roof timbers rose in place of those that had fallen. Songs echoed from the church windows far into the countryside, songs of praise... A new bell summoned the new monks to prayer...

The man who had once seen that beautiful child in the monastery garden could not forget it. He had grown old, yet he was obsessed with the longing to look once more upon that lovely face. He tried to model in wax the features he had once seen in his youth. Again and again he pressed his fingers into the wax, striving to catch the likeness he remembered so well.

Even though in the course of years he made so many waxen images, innumerable faces, he could not catch the likeness he had seen all those years ago.

Until one day...

Again the monk was trying to copy in the soft wax the charming features that he bore in his mind.

Over and over again he shaped the wax, seeking the face of long ago in its transformations.

And suddenly day seemed to break. He was bathed in a clear light.

Again he saw the child.

It stood before him, and it was smiling.

"I am here so that you may finish your little statue."

With trembling fingers the monk started feverishly to shape the wax, trying as exactly as possible to copy the being that stood before him.

In all those years the child had not changed at all. Though it seemed to the monk even more beautiful.

His fingers danced in the warm wax, yet it seemed as if the monk was not modelling it, as if it were fashioning itself, helping the man's fingers, so that the statue should be a faithful likeness of the child.

At last the work was completed...

Next day his brethren found the monk lying motionless.

He was lying beside a statue. An exquisite little statue...

When he had caught the likeness of the heavenly child, he had died. Even from the sleep of death he smiled. As if he were still gazing into the face of that child. Into the face of goodness, the face of hope. Eternal hope.

The face of love...

HOW THE PRAGUE CHILD JESUS
CAME TO PRAGUE

am giving you the most precious thing I have...
Those were the words said by a noble lady to Prior Ludvík. She came into the Church of Our Lady Victorious in the Little Quarter, which belonged to the bare-footed Carmelites. She was Madam Polyxena de Lobkowicz, and she said these words in 1628. And in her arms she carried something wrapped in a white cloth.

What was that most precious, dearest gift brought by one of the richest noblewomen in the kingdom? What was the present she embraced?

The Prior bent in wonder towards Madam Polyxena de Lobkowicz as she unwrapped her gift.

A statue. A tiny little statue.

Madam Polyxena had decided to bring the miraculous little statue of Jesus from her private chapel to where it could be worshipped by all the people of Prague.

The statue of Jesus, made long ago by an old Spanish monk, had found its way to the Bohemian capital city to the Carmelites. From then on it was to link its two homelands, Spain and Bohemia.

What memories may have run through Madam Polyxena's mind on the day she gave the statue to the Carmelites? Thoughts of her mother – Dona Maria Maximiliana Manriquez de Lara y Mendoza? The young Spanish girl married Madam Polyxena's father, Lord Vratislav of Pernštejn, a Bohemian nobleman, and after her wedding she – a member of one of the most famous noble families of Aragon and Castile – left her native sunny Spain for chilly Bohemia, bringing with her one of her wedding presents – the statue of the little Jesus.

Surely Madam Polyxena must have remembered her Spanish mother on the day she gave the figure of the little Jesus to the Carmelite Prior.

The painter Sanchez Coello has preserved for us the likeness of the Spanish noblewoman and her little daughter Polyxena. They are holding hands in the portrait and the faces of both show their intelligence and kindness. At the time it was made they must both have been adorers of the divine child. The worship of Jesus spread very rapidly in Spain, promoted by St. Theresa de Jesu. It is said that whenever she was to go on a journey, she never set out without a statue of the little Jesus, similar to Polyxena's.

And Madam Polyxena surely remembered too the day when her mother gave her the statue - she too received it as a wedding present. That was in 1587, when the beautiful Polyxena married the most powerful of the Bohemian noblemen, Lord William of Rožmberk, a man who almost became the king of neighbouring Poland... And Madam

Polyxena's little statue still accompanied her when, after Rožmberk's death, she married the supreme chancellor of the Bohemian kingdom, Zdeněk Vojtěch de Lobkowicz.

Now the statue of the child Jesus had two homes, two ancient Christian kingdoms, Bohemian and Spanish.

Madam Polyxena had knelt before the statue as a child, as a bride, as a young woman. And now, before deciding to retire to her mansion in Roudnice nad Labem and abstain from the bustle of the world, she knelt before it for the last time in the family chapel of her palace in Hradčany.

It is said that Madam Polyxena knew the miraculous power of the little statue very well, and that is why she decided not to hide it in her private chapel. In the year when her first husband died after twenty-five years of marriage, she dedicated a monastery to the statue. Who knows if Madam Polyxena had not the divine child to thank for her own only child. It was born to her only in her second marriage and at an age when neither she nor her severely sick husband any longer hoped for an heir...

And that only son founded a mighty patriotic and art-loving family that still lives today.

She decided to leave the little Jesus, who had bestowed such benefit on her family, to the people of Prague.

"The little Prague dweller" he was to be called.

The merciful Prague Child Jesus...

"I am giving you the most precious thing I have. Pay honour to this statue and you will fare well."

The Carmelite Prior bowed. He took the statue from Madam Polyxena's hands and placed it in the oratory.

Madam Polyxena and he both clasped their hands in prayer.

The light of a candle flickered across the white face of the Prague Child Jesus, it looked as though the child were smiling.

The Prague Child Jesus had found a home – the place where it was to be at home for the coming centuries.

Madam Polyxena had finished her prayers, but she could not make up her mind to leave the church. For the last time she gazed emotionally into the face of the Christchild.

The child was the same as when Polyxena had prayed to it as a timid bride... As she looked at it now she no longer felt like an ageing woman, twice widowed, approaching the end of her life, but once more like a child, the child that had knelt before this statue so many times with her mother. If what we believe in does not age, we do not age either. Youth is not in the number of years, but in how close we are to God.

For one last time Madam Polyxena's eyes met the eyes of Jesus.

How many people will meet the eyes of this little Child Jesus over the coming centuries, how many million people will kneel before the merciful child, whispering their prayer to him?

* * *

Madam Polyxena left the church. The sound of her footsteps died away. The church fell silent.

The Carmelite Prior extinguished the candle by the Child Jesus and went away.

But a light glowed into the darkness.

A dazzling spiritual light. A light that for many centuries to come was to shine forth from Prague to all continents...

Shining Tracks

A never ending throng
passes throughout the centuries
before the face of the Child

A never ending throng
of children
who grow old
and depart beneath the clay canopy

How many footprints
have remained after pilgrims
who have gone from this world

How many footprints
of those millions
live on
when they have left?

Oh Prague Child Jesus
grant
that at least one of our footprints
remains here
and shines
and gives warmth

Grant life
to at least one of our
footprints

THE TALE
OF THE PRAGUE CHILD JESUS
AND SAINT THERESA THE GREAT

isten to the tale of how the Merciful Prague Child Jesus came to Bohemia.

In the Church of Our Lady Victorious, where the Prague Child Jesus is looked after, a beautiful altar has stood ever since 1667, opposite the altar of the Child Jesus. And it seems that there is some special intention in the placing of this altar, for from it – from the altar of St. Theresa – the Merciful Prague Child Jesus can be well observed.

According to a family tradition that still lives on in the ancient family of the lords of Lobkowicz, the Prague Child Jesus was originally a gift from the very hand of Theresa of Avila. And it is well known that St. Theresa deeply revered Jesus's childhood, so it is no wonder that worship of the infant Jesus came to Bohemia just from Spain, the country where the great saint lay in her cradle.

The young Spanish girl Maria Manrique de Laura was to go to Bohemia as a bride... to leave her home for a distant, unknown country. What would her life be like there? In a country where she knew no one, where no one spoke her mother tongue?

The young Spanish girl knew that her future husband, Vratislav of Pernštejn, was a noble man and one of the most powerful in the Bohemian kingdom. And yet the poor girl was filled with anxiety, she was to leave everything she knew, her country, her family, her language... She was beset with care and the beautiful bride spent many hours kneeling before the family altar, whispering prayers...

Into that old story of anxiety and hope the bride's mother enters, she gives the Spanish girl her own little Jesus – a gift of the family statue for her long journey, the statue that the bride's mother had received from St. Theresa of Avila.

And suddenly the old story begins to sound like a poem... it shows us two women, the ageing mother and her daughter. For a moment they meet, they kneel together before the Merciful Child Jesus, for a moment their two voices in prayer sound in unison, voices full of love. The voice of the ageing woman and the fresh voice of the girl.

Then the girl takes the little Jesus into her arms. Once more she thanks her mother for her gift and in tears they part.

Probably the location of the altar of St. Theresa on the evangelical side of the church recalls tradition. The holy poetess symbolically approaches close to the Child Jesus, the gift she gave to the world through the medium of the land of Bohemia.

The Light in the Church
of Our Lady Victorious

The Prague Child Jesus
shines in the dark church with a glow
like the sun

Every heart
may become
a sun

Sometimes a touch
is enough

The touch of light
ignites a light
in the heart

Oh shining Child
touch our hearts

Or give us words
that with them we may touch
the hearts of our dear ones

Today

The shining Child smiles

"Why do you want those words from me?
Do you not know them?"

THE FIRST MIRACLES

et us set out along the path of the Prague Child Jesus, a path of adventurous, moving events, let us set out into the world of old Prague stories and legends...

Let us follow the path of the Prague Child Jesus through the centuries, a path that touched on ingratitude and respect, humiliation and glory, love and hatred.

The monks kept the statue of the little Jesus, donated by Madam Polyxena, in their oratory and the novices held two-hour-long services before it every day. A great power came from the statue, breathing strength into them. And so that the ordinary people of the Little Quarter might feel the effect of the miraculous child, the monks took the little statue into the church as well. The first admirers of the Prague Child Jesus came to the church, knelt before the child and uttered their pleas.

And the Prague people needed comfort and support in those days. It was a time of war, the Thirty Years' War – one of the cruellest and longest wars that had ever afflicted the Bohemian kingdom. Death, murders, sickness, famine and suffering had taken the place of the years of prosperity and peace known to the previous generation.

The serene and happy Bohemian land – Bohemia Felix, as it was called – one of the richest and most august countries of Europe, became a place of scorched earth, sadness and death.

And just at that time, when so many men, women and children were suffering so much, the Child Jesus came into the Church of Our Lady Victorious. Help came into that world of distress. The Child in the Church of Our Lady Victorious came to give comfort to desperate souls.

Shortly after the Prague Child Jesus had been gives to the Carmelites the first miracles began to take place – the amazed people of Prague told the monks of how their wishes had been fulfilled through the intercession of the Child Jesus. They heard extraordinary testimonies.

The Little Quarter had become a site of miracles.

The sick were healed as in the days of the gospels...

Those sho had not heard their own prayers spoken to the Child Jesus found that their hearing was returned. Those who had been unable to see the Child they prayed to were astounded, their sight came back. And those who had with difficulty hobbled to the church on crutches laid them aside and walked out of the church without pain...

The tidings of the Prague Child Jesus began to spread from Prague, farther and farther, more and more quickly, his fame was borne throughout the kingdom of Bohemia. It grew and strengthened as the glow of the rising sun touches an ever grater area of the Earth.

The Holy Child of Prague

The world is judged by a child
The child needs no code of law
witnesses
or jury

It examines a single point
"How have you
loved me?"

In the answer to this question
lies all

Just one thing is punishable:
to betray love

The world is judged by a child

"How have you
loved?"

GRACIOS: IESULUS.

Balzer ex. Lßæ. et Praga.

TIMES OF WAR

hey were no days of peace and calm that awaited the merciful Prague Child Jesus in the Church of Our Lady Victorious...

In 1631 Prague was occupied – as so many times before – by the German army. The town was pillaged. Soldiers looted the Carmelite monastery, nor did they even spare the church.

The miraculous statue did not waken their respect. One of the vandals dragged it from the altar, broke its arms and hurled it behind the altar.

The German soldiers stole the ecclesiastical gold and silver, but the most precious thing of all remained in the church. Gratiolus Jesulus, the merciful Prague Child Jesus quietly lay crippled behind the altar. It was not the first time, nor even the last, when He who brought help and comfort suffered human hatred and malevolence.

When the Saxon army departed and the monks again took over the ransacked church, the little Jesus lay forgotten behind the altar.

And again evil times fell upon the monastery. Again armies attacked Prague, and again the monks had to leave the monastery. They knew that only death would await them there.

Even when they returned Prague's suffering did not end. The city was afflicted by a terrible plague, such as there had never been within the memory of man, a plague that entered history as "the great plague of Prague". Whole families died out, whole tribes. More and more graves were filled in the cemetery round the church. It is reckoned that many more than half the inhabitants of Prague died at that time. Among them was the Carmelite Prior.

Those who survived used to meet in the plundered church. There they sang and prayed. Their gaze turned to search for their dear ones who had been coming to church with them for years – parents, husbands, wives, children... But the places where they used to sit, to sing and pray, were empty.

Each mass was attended by fewer and fewer people...

The number of graves in the Prague graveyards increased so rapidly that the grave-diggers scarcely had time to dig them.

And death came again and again and opened the doors of Prague houses. One after another it opened them and it seemed it would never stop.

Those who came to the Church of Our Lady Victorious to pray for their dear ones, alive and dead, looked sorrowfully at the place where they had been used to seeing "the little Prague dweller". Their Prague Child Jesus.

If only He were here and would raise his hand in blessing over us.

But the damaged altar was empty.

A Song on the Prague Child Jesus

The Child raises its hand
over the darkness of the heart
in blessing

There breathes into the dusk
a timid light

Only he
who wipes the tears of strangers
will not weep

There breathes into the dusk
an agate light

Only he who shines
lives not in darkness

There breathes into the dusk
a glowing certainty

Only he who never deserts
will not be
deserted

THE MONK FROM LUXEMBURG

he family of the greatest Bohemian sovereign, King of Bohemia and Roman Emperor, Charles IV came from Luxemburg. And some three centuries later a young monk came to Prague from Luxemburg. He certainly had no idea that his name too would live on for hundreds of years. This name was Mikuláš Schockvilerg, and in his order he took the name of Father Cyril a Matre Dei.

Father Cyril was one of the novices who had felt the strength that emanated from the Prague Child Jesus and had held daily services before it.

The chaos of war had then driven him for a long time from his new home in the Carmelite monastery in the Little Quarter. Only in 1637 did he return to Prague, which was to become his second home.

He entered the Church of Our Lady Victorious. He gazed around that once splendid, beautifully decorated church, now ransacked and derelict. And Father Cyril wondered where the Child Jesus was. He wandered through the monastery and the church, sure that the miraculous little statue must be there somewhere...

And at last he really did find it, thrown behind the altar. No longer was it the glittering little figure, so well cared for by Madam Polyxena, that he had remembered well throughout his years of exile. What Father Cyril now held in his hands was a sad wreck of that figure, covered with dust, in a bedraggled blue dress.

Father Cyril pressed the Child Jesus to his breast. He stood it in its old place, knelt down and prayed to it. For a long time he prayed, for his dear ones, for the monastery, for Prague, for all who were suffering, who were losing hope in those harrowing times in many places in Europe.

He prayed for the children, the most helpless beings... He prayed for the Bohemian land, again being approached by a vast army of mercenaries who would steal and murder there. It was then only the end of the first decade of the terrible Thirty Years' War – a further two unending decades were to come.

Father Cyril knelt in the dark church. As a monk he had not even the money to buy a candle and light it on the altar. Only the moonlight streamed into the darkness from the church window.

And suddenly in the silence Father Cyril heard a voice. The voice of a child.

"Have mercy on me and I will have mercy on you."

It is said that Father Cyril was almost struck dumb.

"Give me my arms," the little voice went on, "and I will give you peace. And as you will esteem me, I will visit you."

Father Cyril plucked up his courage and stepped falteringly up to the statue. He pushed aside the blue dress it was clothed in and saw that indeed the figure had no arms. Father Cyril carefully replaced the bedraggled little blue dress and went at once to see the Prior.

He told him of what he had seen and heard. But the Prior did not believe him. And anyway, he said, the monastery had not the money to repair some old broken statue – it might cost as much as a whole gulden...

Father Cyril took the little statue to his cell. And there he prayed for the money to be able to have it repaired. And almost at once it happened that a sick man appeared. He gave not one gulden for the repair of the statue, but a hundred gulden. But even then the Prior's heart was not softened. He did not remember the miracles that Madam Polyxena's gift had performed. He did not believe Father Cyril's testimony. What was the use of a dirty old statue? Instead of it the Prior had a new statue made. But when the monks stood this new statue on the altar a heavy candle fell on it and shattered it to pieces.

Now perhaps, thought Father Cyril, now at last the Prior would have the statue repaired, for what had happened was an omen.

But again the Prior was not convinced.

It seemed to Father Cyril that all his pleas and prayers were in vain. But the moment he lost hope an order came for the Prior to leave Prague. Father Cyril saw his transfer as vis major.

Now at last the Prague Child Jesus would be given the help it sorely needed, he hoped.

For God knows how to make things straight by drawing apparently twisted lines.

The Prague Child Jesus is Waiting

1
I wait
I'm waiting for you –
says the hand raised in blessing
of the dear Prague Child Jesus

Are you troubled? Alone?
Do not fear

Are you dismayed?
Weeping?

I wait
I'm waiting for you

2
Do you wish to be spoken to?
It is so simple
Speak
and you'll be spoken to

For you are what you love

THE MYSTERIOUS LADY

A new Prior came to the Carmelite monastery in the Little Quarter, and Father Cyril visited him immediately.

He told him all he knew about the miraculous little statue. He described the miracles that had taken place years ago in the Little Quarter, when he had been a novice there. He related how he had found the Prague Child Jesus, and about the mysterious voice that had spoken to him.

The New Prior did not believe Father Cyril. In those days there were so many deluded souls wandering through the world, preaching so many strange beliefs. He took Father Cyril for one of them.

Yet the new Prior did decide to try out the power of the little Jesus.

"Very well, I will have the statue repaired, but only on condition that the Prague Child Jesus does something to help our monastery..."

"In what way should he help it?"

"Let him do it some good turn..."

"And has he not already helped so many Prague people?" The words rose to Father Cyril's lips – "Are all those miracles too few?"

But he made no objection and kept silent.

Then he went into his cell. There he prayed for a long time in the dark to the little Jesus, a ray of moonlight shone on the face of the child, the eyes of Jesus looked into those of the monk.

And it is said that then Father Cyril was called into the church, as there was a woman there who wished to speak to him.

There was a woman standing in the dim light of the church. A brightness radiated from her, sublimity, love.

She spoke softly to Father Cyril, saying she did not wish the monastery to suffer want, and she handed the monk money, a great deal of money. And then went straight out of the church, not waiting for a word of thanks.

Who was that woman? Father Cyril had never seen her before and never saw her since. He stood transfixed. There was so much he wanted to say to that sublime lady, but he was unable to speak.

Till his dying day Father Cyril a Matre Dei believed that the hand that gave him the money was the hand of Jesus's mother. For many years Father Cyril believed that the light footsteps, growing fainter as they departed over the stones of his church, were the steps of the Mother of God.

Then Father Cyril ran to the Prior with the money he had received. He told him excitedly what had happened, who had come to the church, who had brought him money for the repair of the statue. THE MOTHER OF GOD.

But even now the Prior refused to believe him. He would perhaps allow half a gulden for the repair of the statue, but a whole one? Certainly not. The monastery had received so much money, but there were more important things that needed doing than mending some old statue.

Disheartened Father Cyril went back to the Christchild.

The monastery had gained so much money at his intercession – yet one single gulden was not to be found to mend that statue.

And once more that childish voice broke the dark silence of the monk's cell: "Stand me at the entrance to the sacristy and you will find a man who will have mercy on me!"

It is written in the monastery chronicle that soon after Father Cyril had placed the statue of the Prague Child Jesus at the door of the sacristy, as he had been told to do, a troubled man came into the church.

He was a Commissar of the imperial army – a man who had seen so much suffering during those long years of war, so many crippled children.

He could not bear the sight of the statue of the divine child in such a pitiful state. He enquired what had happened to it and then at his own expense he had it mended and its arms restored.

The old records show that his sympathy brought him many blessings. The troubles that he had experienced both in his private life and in the army were immediately solved.

At last Father Cyril could look contentedly at the altar. The Prague Child Jesus that had been placed there had both its arms, and it blessed everyone who

came before it. And not only those who approached across the stones of the church. It blessed all
who approached across the bridge of love.

Father Cyril did not doubt that the statue that
stood before him on the altar was miraculous.
Otherwise why would Jesus's own mother have
come herself to the church...?

THE LEGEND OF THE ARTIST
WHO HEALED
THE PRAGUE CHILD JESUS

here are several legends told about the healing of the Prague Child Jesus. They say it was no easy task to give the Prague Child Jesus back his hands, though many sculptors tried to do it. It was not that it was difficult to model the hands of wax. Yet everyone who attempted, to mend the miraculous little statue fared the same. He modelled the arms and hands and fastened them to the body. He showed his work to the monks, took his pay and went away.

But next morning when the monks came to the altar, the picture was always the same: the arms had fallen off the body. The Christchild was in the same state as when they had summoned the sculptor to mend him.

However hard the next sculptor strove, he always fared the same as his predecessor...

They called one artist after another to the church, and each of them tried to make easy money with the work. How simple it seemed to the sculptors to make the arms and hands out of soft wax, so much easier than working with a chisel on marble. Yet it turned out that this job was much more difficult.

Hope came with each new sculptor. He would be the right one who would at last heal the little Jesus. But every morning the new little hands lay on the ground and the Christchild stood armless on the altar above them.

Till one day a young artist applied for the job. No one in Prague had ever heard of him. He had a gentle, boyish face and looked more like a child than a man. He begged to be allowed to try and heal the little statue of Jesus.

What could not be achieved by famous sculptors from Prague and even from far-away countries, the most skilful of the skilled, will certainly not be achieved by this lad, thought the monks. But in the end they did entrust the work to him after all.

The boy knelt down in front of the statue. And he modelled it kneeling, as if he were praying. He touched the wax and the Child Jesus very lightly. It seemed to the monks who were watching that he did not behave like a sculptor. He treated the statue as though he were a doctor and was touching a sick child.

Next day the monks ran impatiently to the church.

And they were delighted.

The Prague Child Jesus had two hands.

And he held them out in blessing, he blessed Prague, he blessed all who came to him...

And the monks considered that none of the previous sculptors had succeeded because not one of them was pure in heart.

Man does not create with the hands or the head alone.

Creation needs the heart.

They came out of the church to thank the sculptor and bestow gifts upon him – but the sculptor had disappeared.

Who was it?

Was it a saint who had come to mend the statue, when for so long the monks had been unable to find anyone to heal the Prague Jesus?

Was it an angel who had flown down to the Church of Our Lady Victorious from paradise to fix the missing arms to the statue with its angelic fingers?

It must have been someone who was pure in heart.

The news of the strange sculptor spread through Prague like wildfire. And the people of Prague ran to the Church of Our Lady Victorious to see at last that their little Jesus was healed.

And the people of Prague reflected on what would have happened if they had been summoned to the Church of Our Lady Victorious to heal the little child. Would one of them have been successful? As they entered the church one after another each of them asked himself this question.

And those who hear this legend ask themselves the same thing, the question has been asked down the centuries: If they asked me to...

The Prague Child Jesus holds out his hand in blessing over all those who ask this question.

And he looks into their hearts...

The Prague Child Jesus' Christmas

On the roofs of Prague
snow floats down
like a great pearly white
orison

Grant us, Prague Child Jesus
that we may ever hear
the words of the Christmas bells:

Still now
still there is time
still now
there's time
to open with love
the door to paradise
still now, still now
there's time

Gratiosus IESULUS apud P.P. Car. Disc.
Micro Pragæ.

THE LEGEND
OF HOW THE PRAGUE CHILD JESUS
SAVED PRAGUE

or centuries the story has been told that the capital city of the Bohemian kingdom owes it to the Christchild that it was not destroyed by the Swedish armies during the Thirty Years' War.

In August of 1639 the people of Prague could observe the enemy soldiers from the towers of their churches and from the hill of Hradčany. The army had surrounded the town and was preparing to attack.

The smoke from the fires on which the soldiers roasted the cattle they stole the Prague people saw as a foretaste of the smoke that would soon rise from their homes. The red glow of the bonfires at night was a prophesy of the conflagration that would destroy their city.

Swedish armies had plundered the Czech lands for years with unprecedented cruelty, they tortured and murdered the people and carried off immense stolen riches. So the Prague people knew very well what awaited them when the enemy mercenaries fell on their homes to the roll of drums...

Terrified people would gather in all the Prague churches. Men, women and children knelt down and prayed imploringly for the protection of their town, for the lives of their dear ones and their own lives.

In the Church of Our Lady Victorious the Carmelite monks held services of pleading uninterruptedly. Day and night the people prayed to the Prague Child Jesus in this church not to let their city perish.

Day and night the Prague people awaited in fear, listening for the gunshots, the drunken cries of soldiers in their streets, the rattle of drums, they expected death, so far camping before their gates, to enter the city walls...

So what was their amazement when one morning they looked out from the castle galleries and saw that the vast army had withdrawn in the night, had disappeared.

They asked the prisoners who had escaped from the retreating Swedes why General Banér, the Swedish commander, had let slip the opportunity of conquering the capital of such a great and famous city. And they were told that during the night of 30th August, the time for which the Swedes had planned the conquest of Prague, a messenger had come to the general who had persuaded him to withdraw.

Again the people of Prague knelt down in gratitude before the Prague Child Jesus. They knelt in the certainty that it was this child, and he alone, who had brought about what they had not dared to hope for, the salvation of their homes.

The Smile of the Prague Child Jesus

People so often wonder
Should I?
Should I not?

Who will advise me?

And yet since the oldest times
there are miraculous scales
to weigh our deeds

The wonderful scales of mercy

The scales of the Prague Child Jesus
weigh everything
against one question:

If I were to do
as I want
would the little Jesus
smile at me?

THE LEGEND
OF COUNTESS ELIZABETH

 et us hear the story of a proud but unhappy woman – a story that has touched
Prague people down the years.

Countess Elizabeth, wife of Count Kolovrat
of Libštejn, fell ill. And her sickness condemn-
ed her to a double suffering – darkness and silence. The rich noblewoman lost both her sight
and her hearing.

Many doctors alternated in the place by her
bedside. The unhappy Count spared no expense.
For a long time he hoped that someone would be
able to help his wife, but in time even he lost that
hope. He would sit sorrowfully beside his wife's
bed, pressing her hand, listening helplessly to her
bitter sobs. He said nothing. She could not have
heard any words of comfort.

If there are no people who can help her – thought
the Count – there is always still a last chance...

There is still Someone who can always help,
who can always see us.

And the Count sent a servant to the Church
of Our Lady Victorious, to beg the monks to bring
the statue of the Prague Child Jesus to his palace.

The merciful Prague Child Jesus left his home.

The Carmelite monks took him into the Count's splendid chambers.

The sick woman got up, desperately grasped the hand of a servant and groped her way through the impenetrable darkness towards the Child Jesus.

She knelt down, reaching out into the blackness that surrounded her. She breathed a prayer into the bottomless silence, the silence that for so long had not been penetrated by a single sound.

The monk placed the Prague Child Jesus in her out-stretched arms and she gently embraced him.

And at that moment she gave a shout.

The darkness around her was shattered by dazzling sunshine, she saw it and realized her eyes could see, the Countess was astonished and listened gratefully to her own voice, choking with happy tears – her ears could hear.

* * *

And the Story goes that the Countess Elizabeth loved the Prague Child Jesus so much that she wanted to keep him in her palace.

Indeed she persuaded the monks to allow the little Jesus to stay in the Kolovrat palace, even though the Countess Elizabeth was to leave Prague. She took a grateful farewell of the statue and entered her carriage, drawn by three pairs of horses.

The coachman cracked his whip – then again and again, the horses pulled with all their might, but the carriage did not move an inch. It stood as though the wheels were rooted in the earth. The coachman urged the horses on again and again, the Count's thoroughbreds neighed, their hoofs struck sparks from the paving stones – but the carriage with the astonished Countess did not even tremble.

The Countess dismounted from the carriage shaking with fear. She understood very well why they could not leave. The Prague Child Jesus was rebuking her for her selfishness.

She should not keep him in her house, he did not belong to her, but to all those who wanted to visit him in the church and make their pleas to him. Countess Elizabeth sent at once for the monk from Luxemburg, Father Cyril.

She told him with shame of what had happened and gave him back the statue of the Prague Child Jesus.

Father Cyril took the Christchild in his arms and carried him back to the Carmelites, to the Church of Our Lady Victorious.

When the Prague Child Jesus touched the altar the carriage moved forward, the six-in-hand drove out of Prague.

And the Prague people's gratitude and esteem for the Prague Child Jesus grew even greater.

THE STORY OF THE PRAGUE CHILD JESUS AND THE THIEF

After the end of the Thirty Years' war the Prague Child Jesus became the best beloved child in Prague...

The poor showed their gratitude for his intercession by giving him their thanks and love, the rich by presents of gold, silver and precious stones.

And the treasures that the Infant Jesus received became a lure for thieves.

There is a story from the year 1702 of a man who decided to seize the gold and gems that had been given to the Prague Child Jesus.

He hid in the church. He was even surprised at how easy he found it, as though the devil himself were helping him. He waited until the last worshippers left the church. Then he waited until the sacristan snuffed out the candles before the altar. He listened for a while – and when there was not a sound of movement anywhere he crept quietly up to the statue, softly lit by the eternal flame.

The little crown on the Christchild's head sparkled as if he had a star in his hair.

A single movement would be enough – and the golden crown will be mine. A single moment would be enough and I can grab all those jewels that surround the Prague Child Jesus, the gifts of those whose entreaties have been heard...

The thief stretched out his hand to the coronet glittering on the child's head – and at that moment he heard a voice. The same voice that had been heard by the monk in far-away Spain as he shaped the soft wax, the same voice that had been heard by Father Cyril a Madre dei. The clear voice of a child. And that voice said into the darkness of the church:

"I am Jesus whom you are harming."

At that moment the thief could not move the hand that reached out to Jesus's crown. He wanted to run away, but he could not move his feet. He wanted to cry out, but he could not move his tongue. He stood there transfixed, like one of the statues that decorated the church...

That is how the monks found him, paralysed, with his sacriligious hand reaching for the face of Jesus.

They considered what they should do with him. And they thought that there was only one way they could help a man so tortured by fear – to ask the Prague Child Jesus to have mercy on him.

And the Prague Child Jesus heard their prayer. As soon as they had spoken it the man could move again.

And the news of the power of the Prague Child Jesus spread round Prague like lightning. People ran to the church to make sure that the thief had really not harmed their "little Prague-dweller".

THE LEGEND
OF THE ENEMY INVASION

uring the Thirty Years' War the luck turned sometimes to one side and sometimes to the other. But the people of Prague suffered whichever side it was that occupied their city, the soldiers had but one aim: to plunder.

And it is told how at one time Prague was occupied by an army that treated its people as enemies, killing them and pillaging.

But the Child Jesus found he had very strange admirers. The general who commanded the enemy army issued an order that none of his soldiers was to harm the Carmelites, indeed he even had the church and the monastery guarded. And the monks made use of this for the benefit of Prague – they opened the monastery gates to the people, many of whom found shelter within the monastery with their families and their possessions. And so they were saved from the murdering and thieving soldiers.

But how were the monks to find food for a monastery so full of refugees? How could they satisfy them?

Twice every day the Brothers gave food and drink to all who had found shelter under their roof. And they did not cease to pray to the Merciful Child Jesus that the army would withdraw, that the Prague people would survive and would not die of hunger.

And then something inexplicable happened.

Even though the Brothers in the kitchen were cooking meals ceaselessly for so many hungry men, women and children, the modest supplies they had had in the monastery grew no less. The occupation of Prague continued, the mercenaries were still ravaging the town, but those who had taken refuge with the Carmelite monks still lived in safety and still had enough to eat and drink.

Every morning the cook woke filled with fear that the supplies would come to an end and the people would go hungry. But every morning he saw that the stocks of food were just the same as when the monastery had first opened its gates to the suffering people of Prague.

And the monks remembered the miracle of the loaves and fishes, and they were filled with joy and gratitude.

After all, it is natural, they thought – for how could the Prague Child Jesus allow those who worship him and whom he loves to suffer?

At last the enemy army withdrew, the people of Prague scattered from the shelter of the monastery to their homes. And they remembered for long how the little Jesus had not let hunger decimate those who had sought refuge beneath his childish hand, raised in blessing.

Das gnadenreiche JESU Kindlein bey denen bar-
füssigen Carmelitern in der kleinen Stat.

The Silence of the Holy Child

In the Church of Our Lady Victorious
silence does sing

In that silence
we meet again
all of those
whom we have loved

In that silence
we meet again
all of those
who have loved us

And are no more

No more?

Every silence
does sing:

Those dear ones whom you love
will never desert you
They have gone
only to remain for ever

Death
is only
where there is no love
No one has died
while your love still lives
Weep not
but love

THE LEGEND OF THE PRAGUE CHILD JESUS AND THE GREAT PLAGUE OF PRAGUE

 eath strode through the capital city of the Bohemian kingdom brandishing its scythe like the most assiduous harvester.

In the Carmelite monastery too one monk after another took to his bed, deserting the sufferers they had been helping, themselves lying down to die in their cells.

It was the custom for the monks to serve midnight mass before the statue of the Prague Child Jesus. And usually after that, all night till the very morning, one of the monks remained praying before the altar of the Child Jesus...

Now the monks lay in their cells, the Christchild was left alone. Only the Prior was well. He was the only one the plague avoided.

Day and night the Prior left the monastery and went into the town visiting the sick, at night he was awake at the bedside of his monks. Sleep came to him seldom and briefly – he could not indulge in sleep when there were so few who could help the suffering. So he again and again left the monastery to give comfort.

One day as he was returning from the streets of the Little Quarter he noticed there was a light blazing in the church.

The sacristan must have forgotten to extinguish the candles, he thought, and went into the sacristy, took the snuffers and stepped into the church.

The altar was bathed in light. It was as if the globe that the Child Jesus holds in his left hand had turned into a glowing summer sun. The light of the altar candles had faded like the glitter of fireflies at noon in August.

At the altar the Prior saw seven figures. They seemed to be woven of the rays of the sun, and they were kneeling before the little Jesus and praying... The Prior could see their shining wings. Angels.

The Prior knelt down and prayed for a long time with the angels. Then he quietly left the church. He hesitated as to whether he should not call someone to the altar, to show him the heavenly guests, but then he thought they should not be interrupted.

Next day he sent the sacristan to change the candles on the altar – they must have burnt down during the night, when they had lit the church for so long. But the sacristan came to tell him that the candles were whole. Not only had they not burnt down, but those that had been short the day before had grown to their original height.

And it is related that the angelic guests came often to pray in the church, they were observed many times surrounding the Prague Child Jesus, and many times the people of Prague saw a glow coming from the windows of the Church of Our Lady Victorious, a heavenly glow, radiated by their winged figures...

Soon after the angels' prayers, witnessed by the Prior, the Great Plague of Prague came to an end. And it is told that that night when the angels knelt before the Prague Child Jesus and prayed, the dying Carmelite monks became well and many other Prague people too grew well on that magical night.

THE LEGEND OF THE VINEYARD

There used to be a vineyard behind the Carmelite monastery in the Little Quarter. Ever since the days of the Bohemian king and emperor Charles IV, who had the most precious French vines brought to Bohemia, excellent wine had been cultivated in the kingdom.

But when the Carmelites took over the monastery the vineyard had been laid waste by war and scarcely survived, only here and there a few sour little grapes appeared on the uncultivated bushes.

Those were days of misery and famine.

Day and night crowds of Prague townspeople came to pray to the Prague Child Jesus. Their godly songs emanated from the Church of Our Lady Victorious over the devastated city.

But where were the Carmelite brothers to find wine for the mass?

The days of war had made every scrap of bread precious in Prague, and wine was a rarity, it was the first thing the plundering soldiers always reached for. And the armies plundering Prague were numberless.

The Brother who tended the garden went to look at the vineyard behind the monastery, but he said to himself that even if he were to plant new seedlings it would take years before there was any wine.

He went to the altar of the Merciful Child Jesus and prayed that the vines he was going to cultivate should be fruitful, so that one day the church should have wine for the mass from its own vineyard.

In the spring, when he went to the vineyard to dig up the old bushes, he was transfixed.

The barren little bushes were transformed, they had grown taller and younger, had put forth emerald stars of leaves as if from the best cultivated of vineyards.

The monks gathered in the vineyard in amazement. Who could remember any vineyard growing up so beautifully, all by itself?

The people of Prague came to gaze at the Carmelite vineyard and they could not believe their eyes, day after day the vines were covered with the biggest and most beautiful grapes that any of them had ever seen. It was as if angels flew down to the Carmelite vineyard at night and looked after the vines, watering the bushes with dew from paradise.

That year there was a glorious harvest in the Carmelite vineyard. They were no longer worried in the church as to where the wine for mass was to come from, their own vines gave them plentiful supplies.

Nor did the monks keep all the wine just for their own mass. They gave it around to all the parishes of Prague. And so it was that wine was used for the mass in Prague that had perhaps been watered by the angels themselves with heavenly dew.

The Hand of the Prague Child Jesus

You raise
your hand and bless
longing

Oh Prague Child Jesus
grant
that we may know
who is waiting for our hand
for our proffered hand

For centuries
it will lie motionless
like a shrivelled hand of those buried
in the crypt

Today
we are able to
give it
Who is waiting for it? Today?

AN ACCOUNT OF THE FACE
OF THE PRAGUE CHILD JESUS

mericus a Santo Stephano left us the first important book on the story of the Carmelite monastery and the miracles of the Prague Child Jesus. In this book, which was published in the Czech language in 1749, there are a multitude of testimonies and an account of the face of the Prague Child Jesus.

Father Emericus a Santo Stephano, Prior of the Carmelites, admits here that he was himself fascinated by the changes in the face of the Child Jesus. – "...I myself, who am writing, in order to fathom the true facts, frequently posed unexpected questions to various persons as to how the picture of the little Jesus appeared on that day, and I received from all an identical reply: frowning and angry. And then on another day: filled with lovingkindness. As those whom I asked could not hear or know of one another, these frequent identical replies did assure me of the trustworthiness of the strange transformations of the face of the picture of our little Jesus."

It was as if the Prague Child Jesus changed his expression according to who was looking at him

...as if he not only saw everybody, but at the same time looked at each as he deserved...

Father Emericus a Santo Stephano tells of a woman who heard of the fame of the Prague Child Jesus and decided to visit him. "...she entered the chapel and looked towards the little Jesus but, to her amazement and horror, she beheld his clothes, but could see neither his face nor the crown upon his head, but instead something black, like a thick cloud: she was as if struck by thunder and, smitten with a terrible fear, did start to tremble all over her body. Soon though she realised the reason – the many wicked sins she had committed over a number of years without shame or true confession, pouring wrong into herself like water; whereupon she repented of her sins, confessed truly and made a sincere resolution to improve her whole life."

"Behold a miracle!" cries Father Emericus a Santo Stephano. The black cloud around the Christchild disappeared – but the woman "sunk deep in sin as she was" could not yet see Jesus's kindly face. Anxiously she returned to the confessional. On the priest's advice she made a general confession. Then when she hurried to the chapel and looked at the Child Jesus she saw his "most lovely face". But she gazed at it only for a while and soon again a black cloud covered his face. In tears the woman begged Jesus to enlighten her, whether perhaps in her confession she had not forgotten some deadly sin – and she remembered such a one. She hastened back to the confessional and there rid herself of that forgotten sin as well... On returning to the chapel she looked fearfully into the face of Jesus – she saw his face. He was smiling at her.

Father Emericus a Santo Stephano writes that the woman declared all this to her priest and confirmed it with a vow.

Every day pilgrims enter the Church of Our Lady Victorious.

Every day they look into the face of Jesus.

Is he smiling?

Or frowning?

Is his face visible?

We follow in the footsteps of the baroque pilgrims.

But the way we take to the face of Jesus is our own way.

Song to the Prague Child Jesus

Oh Prague Child Jesus
I beg you
may I see the world
not with my own eyes
but with yours

May I see the hearts
around me
not with my own eyes
but with yours

The greatest gift
is to see gifts with the eyes of the Child

THE HOME
OF THE PRAGUE CHILD JESUS

here should we start the tale of the place that has for centuries been cherished by the Merciful Prague Child Jesus?

We will begin with a report from a great distance... One of the Czech women who worship the Prague Child Jesus told of how when she was staying in South America, in Colombia, she took an interest in the lives of the poorest of the poor...

One of those she often met was an old Red Indian woman who used to bring her flowers and often stopped to talk. One day the Czech woman told the Red Indian woman that the day was coming near when she would have to leave for Prague.

"That is a beautiful town," said the old woman dreamily.

The Czech woman was astonished ... how could an illiterate woman from the other side of the world know her town and know that it was beautiful?

"HOW COULD IT NOT BE BEAUTIFUL, WHEN IT IS THE CITY OF THE CHILD OF GOD?"

She knew of Prague through the Prague Child Jesus. And like her vast crowds of believers in distant continents know of it through him. It is said that many inhabitants of remote corners of the world know only the name Prague from the whole of Europe – because of the Prague Child Jesus.

The old Red Indian woman from distant Colombia, like many of her countrywomen, believed that the little Jesus used to go to school in Prague. And she believed that Prague was a neighbouring town to Jerusalem.

Prague in their minds is steeped in poetry.

So many travellers to far-away places have had similar experiences as that Czech woman in Colombia – for the natives of those lands Europe is a hazy idea, but Prague, the home of the Prague Child Jesus, is inscribed in their minds and hearts.

Prague is famous in nearby countries and those far away, it is famous because of the Divine Child – his picture is clasped by Red Indians in their boats during storms on Lake Titicaca, his name is whispered by an Indian who is mortally ill, it is breathed in prayer by a Chinese peasant, sung by children on the Pacific islands... it is touching to listen to the testimonies that reach Prague.

Thanks to the Merciful Prague Child Jesus the fame of Prague has spread throughout the world, thanks to him it has become THE CITY OF HOPE for so many believers.

So let us pay a short visit to Prague, the capital city of the ancient and famed kingdom of Bohemia, now the capital of the Czech Republic.

Let us visit the home of the Prague Child Jesus...

This is not the place to speak of the history and the beauties of Prague, a city admired by pilgrims for a thousand years, a city that ranks amongst the most beautiful in the world.

Let us only mention that every architectural style is inscribed in the face of this city – each of them has contributed to its splendour. Experts know Gothic Prague, baroque, Art Nouveau – each style has adorned Prague with wonderful churches.

Prague is known as the city of a hundred spires which, it has been said, amounts to saying "godly Prague". Innumerable towers, turrets, domes of Prague churches characterize the panorama of the city, over which rises the magnificent Gothic cathedral, the work of "the Father of his Country" – the Bohemian king and Holy Roman emperor Charles IV (1311–1367), one of the greatest and most godly of medieval rulers.

And where in Prague, that "mater urbium" – mother of towns – is the place where the Prague Child Jesus lives?

Let us enter his home for a moment...

Let us enter the ancient Church of Our Lady Victorious. One of the best-known churches of the whole Catholic world is to be found in one of the most delightful quarters of Prague, the Little Quarter.

Let us approach this baroque church... At the height of the gable we see a star. This is the motif of Stella maris, the sign that we are entering a Marian church. But the motif of the star also links the Carmelite monks with their sign of the sea star, the Mother of God. And the order of the barefoot Carmelites has it in their emblem.

Wahre Abbildung des neuen Altars welcher zu Ehren des gnadenreichen Jesuleins bey denen P.P. barfüßige Carmeliten in der Residenz kleinen Stadt Prag A. 1776 von seinen andächtigsten Verehrern, zum dankbaren Denkmal prächtig aus Marmor errichtet worden ist. Auf Kosten der Sommischen Buchhandlung vorlege.

And it was the Carmelite monks who looked after the Prague Child Jesus from the moment they received the little statue from Madam Polyxena de Lobkowicz.

As if it were a symbol: the victorious Jesus is worshipped in the church of his mother, Our Lady Victorious.

We see the statue of the Mother of God even before we enter the church, on the baroque sandstone portal. She looks at everyone who comes to her son.

As soon as we pass through this lofty portal we find ourselves in a baroque world, a world of innermost spiritual piety and poetry.

The church dating from 1611, originally Protestant, was built by the Italian architect Giovanni Maria Filippi of Dosindo, a famous builder at the court of the emperor Rudolph II. This emperor, one of the greatest art lovers to sit on the throne and perhaps the greatest art collector anywhere, made Prague in his day the capital of European art. He summoned reputed artists to his court from all over the world.

He was especially fond of Giovanni Maria Filippi and made him head of the imperial building office. He even became his son's godfather. Filippi's works were the gateway to the new architecture that was coming into the country – baroque architecture. And Filippi may be called "the master of Marian churches". For this was not the only one he built, there were many others, and his work influenced that of other architects. His name takes its place in the history of Czech architecture. He created, for instance, that charming monument in the Labe valley, the Church of the Virgin Mary in Stará Boleslav, the place where the martyr's death of St. Wenceslas, patron saint of the Czech Lands, is commemorated...

It seems as if the Prague Child Jesus, long before Madam Polyxena gave his statue to the Carmelite monks, had chosen the greatest architect in the Czech Lands for his church.

And if the metaphor "the father of Czech baroque churches" has been used in this church, it has been used rightly, for this church inspired the form of so many Czech baroque churches.

Art historians point out the similarity of the church facade with that of churches in Rome (Santa Trinita dei Monti) and in Madrid (Church of St. Andrew). It is thought that this similarity was the wish of the Carmelite monks, who in this far northern land recalled their own country, and also the wish of the churches maecenas, Don Baltasar de Marradas, an imperial general who came from Spain, but settled permanently in Bohemia. Marradas's coat of arms decorates the church facade, and it is interesting that part of this coat of arms is formed by the emblem of Lara de Manrique, whose family Madam Polyxena's mother came from, and who was also related to the Spanish general.

A detailed description of the church can easily be found in the guidebooks, which write of the wonderful chapels, the miraculous pictures. Of these last we may mention the famous picture of the Virgin Mary of Mantua, whose fame centuries ago equalled that of the Prague Child Jesus.

Wahre Abbildung des Anmuthigen Jesuleins, so in dem Chor deren W.
W.E.E. Geistl. Klosterfrauen. Ord. Ass. H.V. Dominici bey S. Jaura bei der
Romoldstatt stall Prag von etlich 100 Jahr hero, andächtig verehret wird

The guidebooks tell of the beautiful altars on the evangelical side of the church and those on the epistolary side, of the main altar with the patron saints of the Carmelite order, also the admirable masterpieces of the great Czech baroque painter Petr Brandl and many other works of art.

But here we shall stop only at the most famous altar of the whole church – a marble altar from 1667. This is the place that is the target of prayers, day and night, from all continents.

Here is the altar of the Prague Child Jesus.

The divine Child shines into the dusk of the church from a lovely glass cabinet. Twenty silver angels surround the little Jesus. The statue is standing in a silver case that reaches to its waist and protects it from any damage. The Christchild stands on a pedestal in which a great ruby shines in the form of a heart and crystals and Bohemian garnets glitter. On Jesus's right hand a golden statue of the Virgin Mary glows and on his left one of St. Joseph. Over the altar of red and grey marble there is a statue of God the Father, as if guarding the Child Jesus from heaven.

Ten generations have knelt before this altar, ten generations have been granted mercy...

Here we are at the place that is touched every second of time by the prayers of innumerable worshippers of the Prague Child Jesus.

Let us recall only that within this church the paths are linked of many creators and many lovers of the little Jesus from many countries. The statue of the Child Jesus itself came to Prague to believers thanks to a Spanish noblewoman and endowed by a Spanish patron. The church was built by an architect from Italy. And the man to deserve most for the prosperity of the cult of the Child Jesus came from Luxemburg.

There is no room here to write of the art treasures of the church, a detailed guide to the complicated events that have befallen it and its treasures would fill a whole book.

These sentences are merely intended to show that by a special intention of fate the little Prague dweller gained a worthy seat even before coming to the city and that people who had honoured him long, long ago had a share in making his home.

He found his home in the church of his victorious mother.

The Prague Child Jesus is at home in Prague.

And through the numberless prayers that fly to him day by day from all over the world he is constantly linked with the whole world. So that the Prague Child Jesus is really at home in the whole world.

It has been well said that our home is the place we carry in our hearts. And the home of the Merciful Prague Child Jesus is in so many millions of hearts.

The Home of the Prague Child Jesus

1
The place that is our home
can be
whatever we call home

With what a lack of care do people choose
their home

They move from one heart to another
and are the poorer
for each and every move

2
The angel – that the old legend says
flies to the Prague Child Jesus every night –
is amazed

Is there some other home
than the heart of the Child?

When you choose
your home
you choose all

THE MERCIFUL LITTLE STATUE

hat does the Merciful Prague Child Jesus really look like?

Everyone knows of it – from holy pictures, little statues, medallions... But in most of these portrayals the likeness is much changed.

What does the Prague Child Jesus look like seen from close at hand?

Usually the Christchild is portrayed soon after birth. That is how we know him from innumerable mangers in Bethlehem scenes... Or else he is pictured in his mother's arms.

But the Prague Child Jesus on the other hand presents Jesus at the age of two or three years. So far as the child is not clothed in the splendid little robes with which the statue is usually adorned, it has the figure of a slender standing boy. The beautifully modelled body is covered with a long, free-flowing robe that covers the right foot, though leaving the left uncovered. The hands are in that characteristic position that is so well known: the left uplifts a terrestrial globe decorated with a cross. The right gives a blessing with the movement always used by priests in blessing people. The face of the Prague Child Jesus is not like all of its supposed copies, so many of which have for centuries been placed in churches and in devout households. But what was written by one of the Child Jesus' Czech admirers is certainly true:"...the longer our eyes gaze into his face, the more we see that a certain kindness, goodness and gravity flow from it, luring the mind and heart to it and encouraging one involuntarily to fall on one's knees and bow down to that mystery that, for the love of man, God became a poor child, so that he should be entirely like us and in no way different."

The little statue of the Prague Child Jesus is forty-six centimetres high and the pedestal is twenty centimetres high.

For centuries the little Jesus has been adorned according to the taste of the day, as the taste changed so did the fashion. In the Rococo period, for instance, the Child Jesus' little head was given a white wig.

The fame of the little dresses in which the Child Jesus is clothed has spread far abroad. The Carmelite monks now take care of very many of these robes – gifts that have been brought by believers. And the ancient custom is still preserved today of changing the Child Jesus' clothes according to the season.

And how is the Prague Child Jesus dressed?

First white robes are put on the statue, something like priests' albs. This kind of garment for the Child Jesus is based on church tradition. Two of these robes are then covered by a vestment that is like a priest's dalmatic. It is usually made of velvet, brocade or silk. And on top of that again the Child Jesus is given a cloak similar to a pluvial.

The little crown that decorates the divine Child' s head does not lie directly on his head, but is fixed slightly above it. Even though from a distance it looks as though it was resting on the head – but the soft wax might be damaged.

This crown is a gift from Count Bernard Ignác of Martinic, a nobleman from an old Bohemian family, who was the supreme burgrave of the kingdom and was grateful to the Prague Child Jesus for many mercies.

The custom of clothing the Prague Child Jesus comes from ancient times – he was wearing robes even when Madam Polyxena brought the little statue to the Carmelite monks. It is said that the later tradition of donating the little Jesus magnificent materials comes from the time of the great plague. Those who wished to thank the Divine Child for their recovery presented him with jewels and brocades as a symbol of their gratitude. And indeed the dress materials from this time are the most precious – the brocades were woven with gold and silver, the cloaks ornamented with pearls and precious stones. They bear witness to the love of the Czech ladies and maidens for the Child Jesus, as they covered his robes with marvellous embroideries.

Many of the festal robes have been preserved, and their styles show the development of fashion. The magnificent, costly baroque clothes are replaced by pink Rococo robes decorated with ribbons and these again by other clothes according to the latest taste.

From baroque times to the present day clothes have constantly been sent to Prague from worshippers of the merciful Prague Child Jesus. Fashions change, the love remains the same...

Let us open the ancient cupboards in which the clothes are kept in the church sacristy.

Lying there is a green velvet gown given to the Christchild by the Empress Maria Theresa, it is decorated with gold embroidery and the story goes that the empress embroidered it herself. Then there is a red robe, also embroidered in gold, dedicated to the Child Jesus by the Emperor Ferdinand. Next we find white dresses decorated with pearls or Bohemian garnets... and so we could go on looking through the treasures given by grateful admirers.

And gifts have come from far-off places, and still do... There is a beautiful robe from the United States of America. And another from China, embroidered with flowers of tender chrysanthemums. And stitched between the chrysanthemums in Chinese are the words: Divine Child Jesus, have mercy on China..." And then there is a further exquisite robe that came from the Philippines...

We turn over more and more gifts...

The tradition started by the baroque admirers of the little Jesus is still alive today.

Which of his robes the Child Jesus will be wearing depends on the time of year you enter the church. They are changed during the course of the year according to the liturgical colours. In baroque times it was pious Prague ladies who saw to the changing of his clothes, then for many years the English Virgins of St. Joseph, now – Carmelite sisters of Infant Jesus.

If you go into the Church of Our Lady Victorious you can see the Merciful Prague Child Jesus in green robes – those given him by the Empress Maria Theresa. He is dressed in them for the festival that bears the name of Jesus. If you visit the Prague Child Jesus at Easter, he will be dressed in white. For Whitsuntide he wears red. A violet robe, less adorned, is used for times of fasting and Advent. But at whatever time you visit the Prague Child Jesus, in whatever colour he shines from the altar, he is always waiting for you with his mercy. He will always raise his hand in blessing...

In conclusion let us quote the words of one of his Prague worshippers:

"Whoever has turned to him with a plea to be heard, for help in physical or spiritual matters, he has always complied, helped everyone, taken all under his protection, never let anyone go away empty-handed. He sheds his mercy not only in Prague, but all over the world, wherever his childhood is worshipped."

Das gnadenreiche Iesus Kindlein
beÿ denen PP. Carmel. in Prag.

Ioan. Georg. Remele feic et excud. A. V.

The Prague Child Jesus Sings

Softly,
You shall hear a song

At every moment
at every moment of distress
the Child will sing

"I am with you"

Softly,
You shall hear a song

At every moment
at every moment of lonesomeness
the Child will sing
"I am with you"

Weep not
You shall hear a song

At every moment
at every moment of despair
the Child will sing
"I love you"

"I am with you
I love you"

"You are not yet so weak
but that you can
wipe away someone's tear"

CENTURIES OF MIRACLES

or centuries believers from Prague and Bohemia have been paying homage to the Prague Child Jesus, and believers from many other countries too. And it is amazing what a vast number of miracles have been experienced by the worshippers of the Prague little Jesus from the seventeenth century until today. There have been so many of those who have been able, with tears of gratitude, to convince themselves of the truth of the words written about the Prague Child Jesus:

"...he will help when all human help seems to be in vain. He will never betray those who trust him."

A whole book could be written about the "Prague miracles", quotations of reports that have accumulated, one beside another, ever since baroque times.

And we only know a fraction of all the testimonies. How many of them were destroyed when, during the reign of the Emperor Joseph II, an enemy of the church, of art and of the Czech nation, documents on miraculous cases of healing, kept in the Church of Our Lady Victorious, disappeared... How many testimonies remained unpublicized during the four decades of the twentieth century, when religious life in Bohemia was suppressed. And how many again remained the secret of those who rejoiced only in their inner hearts at the mercy shown to them and kept silent about God's help.

And how many miracles have taken place all over the world, news of which never reached Prague?

We know that wonder at the might of the Prague Child Jesus filled the minds of Prague people and of pilgrims many centuries ago. Pictures and little figures of the Child Jesus spread rapidly all over Europe and across oceans as well. And the numbers of those who appealed to the "little Prague dweller" increased still more rapidly...

From dawn, when the Church of Our Lady Victorious opened, pilgrims streamed through its doors, and they prayed before the Child Jesus till it grew dark.

In 1739 altogether 2,568 masses were celebrated in honour of the Prague Child Jesus – and his fame and glory were still to grow...

Let us look through the reports of extraordinary recoveries, some of the testimonies that emerge from the twilight of oblivion. Let us look at more than three hundred and fifty years of miracles...

* * *

Names, figures, faces, stories come from the half light of ancient times – each one stranger than the last, and all of them, from the oldest to those of the present day, have one thing in common – the most important – a happy end.

One of the earliest reports to have been preserved comes from the time of Father Cyril, a great admirer of the Prague Child Jesus.

From the words that come to us across the distance of the centuries we can sense the anxiety: the Prior of the Carmelites is fatally ill. It seems there is no help for him. But then the monks decide to entrust their prior to the hands of the "heavenly healer", as the help of wordly doctors is in vain. As soon as they brought the little statue of Jesus into the prior's bedroom he felt relief, and soon he was completely well. After being restored to health he took the Prague Child Jesus himself from his bedroom to the chapel, accompanied by the other monks. There he celebrated a solemn mass and dedicated a new chalice and other gifts to the honour of the little Jesus.

From olden days most of the reports of recoveries that have been preserved concern noblemen or outstanding personalities. Reports of miracles affecting simple and unknown people were not considered so important. It is simply stated that there were many, many of them. But if the prayers of a simple Prague citizen were answered it was not so interesting for his contemporaries as if they were speaking of someone famous.

We can give as an example a story that for long excited baroque Prague and was related both in palaces and in the poorest cottages – the story of the healing of Phillip Count Mannsfeld.

Count Mannsfeld came of a Protestant family, but was converted to Catholicism and became an imperial Field Marshal. Old testimonies show us this powerful aristocrat lying on his deathbed in Prague. The best doctors were summoned to his bedside, but all of them had given up hope. However the sick Marshal refused to give in. He too had heard news of the wave of recoveries brought about by the Prague Child Jesus and he began to invoke the Merciful Child. He made a solemn promise in his honour and had several masses served in his own name in the Carmelite chapel. And it happened that on 27th August 1647 "to the great astonishment of the doctors present" the Count recovered.

And much more could be told of the fates of counts and of further mercies granted – there could be hours of talk of other deeds through which the Prague Child Jesus helped his worshippers in baroque days. From the mists of oblivion more and more names, places and stories emerge. And sometimes they are adventurous stories.

One of them shows a ship foundering in the waves, it cannot escape being wrecked. Three Carmelite monks are saved from the ship, but they are in danger of being drowned. They manage to cling to a steep cliff. One of them is Father Ildefons, who in 1737 had been elected general of the Carmelite order. Soon after his election he had set out to make a visitation in Sicily, sailing from Palermo to Milazzo with two other monks. Now that his ship has been sunk he is anxiously watching the rising tide as the waves wash higher and higher up the cliff. The monks too watch the tide and take leave of their lives in prayer.

Father Ildefons came of a Bohemian family, and before his appointment he had been a prior in Prague. He greatly revered the Prague Child Jesus and carried his picture always with him.

And now he invoked him in prayer.

So far only sinister stormy waves had been visible on the sea but now – behold – a boat! It was sailing there by the purest chance and it saved the shipwrecked monks. When he was wrecked Father Ildefons had with him a precious missal, decorated with gold and silver. Water had got into the knapsack in which he carried the missal and everything – except the missal – was soaked. After being saved the general of the Carmelite order sent the missal – so strangely preserved – to the Prague Child Jesus as a gift.

Let us leave the stormy seas of Sicily and return to Prague, to the bedside where the only son of the Countess Buquoy lies suffering. An ancient source describes the immeasurable pain of both the child and his mother. In vain had she called the best reputed doctors to her child. None of the medicaments brought by these best of doctors was of any help. What could the desperate mother do? Give up all hope? She turned for salvation to the Merciful Prague Child Jesus.

The priest celebrated a mass for the child. When it came to the elevation of the Host the sick child felt better and soon it was entirely cured.

Even in the old days people felt they needed to be sure that a testimony was trustworthy, so some of the reports have a seal appended.

And if people in baroque times found the deeds of the Prague Child Jesus incredible, how much more incredible do they seem today?

There is not the space to tell of all the miracles. Which of the old reports should we choose?

Let us choose the testimony of Joseph de Vignet, a famous doctor. On 10th March 1752 his blind child regained its sight after a prayer to the Prague Child Jesus.

From the dusk of the centuries faces look out, names and stories. All of the stories are touching, dramatic – and all of them have similar features: desperation becomes faith, faith becomes prayer and prayer brings a gift.

The miracles are from different centuries – and yet the ancient grief and joy are so much like our own. And the gratitude of long ago is just the same as now.

The centuries of miracles have not ended – here too are reports of miracles from our own century. There is no mention here of counts, the news speak of the ordinary people of today, people of different professions and from different countries...

And often, so very often, they speak of children – so many times the little Jesus has given his gifts just to them.

Miracles happen in the Czech Lands and to the same extent in far distant places.

And now again we see a bed with a sick child, the Czech little boy Vlastimil. The doctors have given up all hope, the mother has sent a telegram to the father to come and see his child. He is on his way. Is he coming for a funeral? At the last moment the mother puts a medallion of the Prague Child Jesus on her son's neck – and the boy comes back from death's door, he is cured.

The son of a count centuries ago, the son of a clerk in our own century – what do they have in common?

Love of the Prague Child Jesus.

We leaf through the testimonies from our own century. How many of them were not recorded, how many did not reach the Carmelite monks in Prague?

Everyone who has received mercy on intercession from the Merciful Prague Child Jesus can write of it to the address:

Klášter Pražského Jezulátka
řádu bosých Karmelitánů
Karmelitská 9
CZ - 118 00 Praha 1
Česká republika (the Czech Republic)
fax: ++42 -2 - 53 07 52

We leaf through the testimonies from our own century that did reach Prague. Which should we choose? The story of the Belgian whose mortally ill wife regained her health after prayers to the Prague Child Jesus? The story of the woman from Chile who inexplicably recovered at the intercession of the Prague Child Jesus? The story of the doctor from the Philippines who came to Prague to give thanks for his son's being saved from death? Should we tell of the Spanish woman who unexpectedly recovered from the results of a car accident? Or a worshipper of the Prague Child Jesus from Madagaskar?

As people have believed since baroque times, all sincere pleas will be heard by the little Jesus.

New testimonies are reaching Prague even today. Just a sheet of notepaper ... a few grateful words ... a report.

We only find out about some mercies many years later. The church door opens and a simple old woman comes in, a Mexican woman of American Indian origin. Forty years ago she became paralysed and could not move. Her head and whole body seemed to be made of stone. She lay unmoving on her bed and prayed for deliverance. Then she had a dream in which the Prague Child Jesus appeared to her. The woman sent a desperate prayer to him, promising that she would go to Prague to thank him for his mercy. And then – she could hardly believe it: she could easily move her head, then her leg... After a time her paralysis passed away. For a whole forty years she dreamt of visiting Prague, but she was so poor that she could not even consider the idea. Only after forty years was she able to collect the money for the journey. At last she opened the church door and saw the shining Child on the altar – the Child she had seen four decades ago in her dream. She knelt down in tears...

From Brazil came a photograph of a smiling girl sent by her grandmother with the news that the girl had been cured at the intercession of the Prague Child Jesus.

Another sheet of paper... An Italian woman confirms that she has recovered from a malignant disease at the intercession of the Prague Child Jesus...

Perhaps one day a fat book will be published bringing testimony to his miraculous power, perhaps one day someone will collect reports of all the mercies that the Prague Child Jesus has shown to his worshippers in our century.

For here we have only glanced through some old and some new testimonies. We have let only a few faces, lives and stories look out of them.

Maybe one day the recorded testimonies will include one from you...

There is one thing that all the reports we read have in common – trust in the Child Jesus and confirmation of that trust.

Love is always greater than hopelessness – love heals.

How should we end this chapter, this account of miracles?

Perhaps the best ending will be a testimony noted down by one of the wardens at the Children's Home in Frýdlant nad Ostravicí:

"Our little six-year-old Hermína was just getting over a severe illness that we had hardly expected her to survive, but as soon as she was almost well she got pneumonia badly. Three of her sisters had died of that illness and her father, whom we called immediately, assumed that it would be her final illness too. The doctor held out no hope, but the children kept on praying. Fever wracked the sick girl, draining her strength, and we did not move from her bedside day or night, just as the children did not move from the dear Prague Child Jesus.

At last it seemed evident that the little girl would not get over her illness. She lay helplessly on the bed, hardly breathing, her mouth open, her body growing cold. Anxiously we asked the doctor if hope was still possible, and he answered: "No, the child is too weak." Then the warden gathered all the children together and said: "You must beg the Little Jesus for Hermína's health." And while a hundred childish hearts prayed in "The Children's Paradise" we waited for the end of our little ward. Then the little girl gave a shout, her body tossed violently, we supposed that her last moment had come – but she began to give signs of life, she breathed more freely, life came back to her cooling limbs, and in a moment we saw that the children's prayers had been heard! When the doctor came the next day he shook his head in amazement at a recovery such as he had never seen. And within eight days the little girl was running about the garden with her friends as if she had never been ill, and not at all like someone who only a week ago had been a certain candidate for death. Such a rapid recovery can hardly be naturally explained, so in "The Children s Paradise" the statue of the dear little Jesus is considered a miraculous one. And here too his promise is fulfilled. "The more I shall bless you, the more will you worship me."

Verses on the Prague Child Jesus

1

Oh sweet Prague Child Jesus
grant that we may wash away
mounds of sorrow
and experience
may
we feel only that childish certainty
Trust in the father

2

The gentle Child
in the Church of Our Lady Victorious
blesses us every second

Why should we fear?

Whoever loves the Child
is victorious

The Prague Child Jesus

1

In the silky dark of the Church of Our Lady
Victorious
the Child glows
the Child of light

The Child knows
there is no need to fear
the night

Darkness
is only light
on which no one has smiled

2

In the silky dark of the Church of Our Lady
Victorious
the Child still glows
the Child of Light

The Child knows
there is no need to fear
the night

Night
is only light
that has been too long alone

Darkness
is light
to which love is unknown

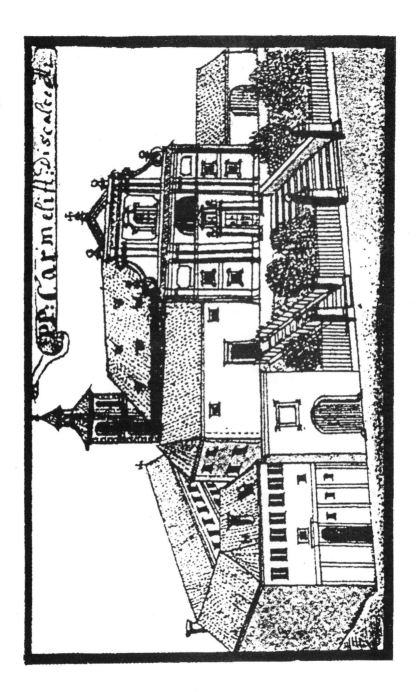

WHY GOD
"THE CHILD"?

P. MARCO CHIOLERIO ocd

1. WHY GOD "THE CHILD"?

St. Anselm, considering the mystery of the Incarnation, begins one of his books with the rhetorical question that runs through the whole of his reflections: "Why God – the Man"? Involuntarily a paraphrase of this question occurs to us, that appeared in a publication issued twenty years ago: "Why God – the Child?" Why have so many devout Christians spontaneously turned with their prayers, songs and pleas always to the little Jesus, Jesus at the beginning of his life, blessing and sometimes holding a symbol of the world in his hand, sometimes snuggling in his mother's embrace. And why was this child usually pictured in royal robes with a crown on its head, whether in pictures or as a statue?

These are not such needless questions as someone might think. The oldest gospel we have is the Gospel of St. Mark. He starts to tell the story of Christ's life from the moment when he was christened by John, known as the Baptist, in the river Jordan. Then too the Gospel of St. John, after a poetic prologue about the meaning of the Word that was made flesh, tells of Jesus' life from about his thirtieth year. So let us quickly go through the biblical texts that will help us to somewhat deepen the initial question and so better understand and experience the feeling of devotion for the Prague Child Jesus.

2. A SON AS A PROMISE OF GOD

ven if we only skim through the pages of the Bible we cannot but notice the importance that is attached to the child, all the more in special circumstances. While it is true that the child was not very highly considered in Jewish society, for instance as a witness in the legal sense or as a religious subject (to the age of twelve)[1], it is also true on the other hand that every child contains within itself the promise of life. Every new individual that came into the world, especially if it was a first-born and a boy, was considered a special gift of God, the living fulfilment of the promise of life, fertility and providence, written in the creative work of the Lord God.

Apart from a slight mention of the child Seth, whom Eve took to be a gift planted within her in place of her son Abel, whom Cain slew[2], the first mention of a child we find if we go through the books of Holy Script in order, is rather in the negative sense: the child is absent. We read of Abraham's wife: But Sarai was barren, she had no child[3]. And then begins the salvation with God's promise that he will give "a son" to Abraham, a seed that will open the history of the salvation of mankind begun from God's free initiative, mankind represented by him who millions of people will come to call "our father Abraham".

The intervention of God opens up the blind alley of Sarai's barrenness, as happens in various similar situations that afflicted families of the chosen nation. We may recall Rebekah, the wife of Isaac[4], Rachel, the second wife of Jacob-Israel[5], the wife of Manoah and mother of Samson[6], Hannah, the mother of the prophet Samuel[7] and so on and so on, until Elizabeth, the last of the barren women, who met the first among virgins, Mary. For all of these women and their husbands a child that is born is a sign of life, of hope, of great joy. But it is not only the joy of the family that is delighted by the new birth, it is a sign of the love of God himself, of his care for all mankind. The child that is born shows that God's promise is much stronger than our closure, sadness, barrenness, helplessness. His love opens new paths, brings back lost hope, returns dignity to those who have been living shut into their pain in hopeless situations[9].

The wealth of the biblical significance of the child does not end with barren mothers. The birth of other children is told of there as of "a miracle", to stress the importance this birth will have in the plans for salvation that God has for all mankind. The child Moses, saved from the water (a symbol of evil) is a child saved from death so that it could lead its nation out of slavery and help it to survive. Moses was chosen to become the head of the nation, chosen by God, to tell the people his name, to let them know who the true Lord is, to acquaint the people with his laws, with his admirable deeds, always carried out for all nations, for mankind, yet using ordinary and simple instruments, as children do.

A child is "a sign of contradiction", he who, as a result of his innocence and often by his mere presence, causes the truth to come to light. Sometimes, through the fact that he "does not speak", he becomes for someone a sign of good, for another a sign of evil, like the son of David and Bathsheba[10]. In that case the child emphasizes the sin of the king, who forgot his humble origin and how, when he was still a boy, he became an instrument of God's might against the Philistine giant Goliath, a symbol of one who believes in his human strength, not the might of God.

The books of the Bible regard with faith those children who become a sign that the Covenant between God and the nation continues. And not only that. A single child, however important in its singleness, also becomes "a collective symbol" and gradually helps the whole nation to call God "father" – something unknown in other religions. From the spirituality of our "elder brothers" the

Jews, we too have inherited this deep intuition: God is our father and we are all his offspring, his "children".

He appointed Moses, and he, feeling the weight of his arduous task, to lead his nation through the desert to the promised land, reproaches God: "Have I conceived all these people? Have I begotten them that thou shouldest say unto me, Carry them in thy bosom as a nursing father beareth the sucking child?"[11]. Here Moses compares the nation to a new-born child, which the Lord himself conceived, which was born of the will of God himself, who is here for the first time considered as the "father" of the nation, of each every one.

This idea was gradually taken over and refined by the prophets. Every time the nation grumbled at God, or at the leaders of the nation who should have represented God, He tried himself to bring "his own son" back to the true path: "Is Ephraim my dear son? Is he a pleasant child? For since I spake against him I do ernestly remember him still," says the Lord through the mouth of the prophet Jeremiah and shows that even he, the Lord, if forced to correct believers, does so unwillingly, like a father who dearly loves his child and punishes him for his own good, though with a heavy heart.[12]

A historical opportunity for one of the greatest prophesies in this sense, which then forms a kind of bridge between the Old and the New Testaments, is the meeting between the prophet Isaiah and King Ahaz, who had come out to control the conduit of the capital city, threatened with a siege.[13] Faced with the king's disbelief in the Lord God –

for the king sought rather a military ally – Isaiah foretells "a sign": "Behold, a virgin shall conceive, and bear a son, and shall call his name Immanuel." The birth of a son to a royal family often meant joy for all the people, who already saw the child as their future king. In the case of the son of Ahaz this was repeated, but the sign was still greater, becoming a certainty of the presence and protection of God for the whole nation, not only in the present but the future as well: "The people that walk in darkness shall see a great light: they will joy before thee according to the joy in harvest, for thou shalt break the yoke of his burden. For unto us a child is born, unto us a son is given, and the government shall be upon his shoulder; and his name shall be called Wonderful, Counsellor, The mighty God, The everlasting Father, The Prince of Peace. Of the increase of his government and peace there shall be no end, upon the throne of David, and upon his kingdom."

This text is especially important, because in a later interpretation, that had witnessed the fall of David's dynasty, the words of promise that there would be "no end" to the government of the "everlasting Father, the Prince of Peace" could not cease with the pious King Ezechiah, who tried to rule better than his father Ahaz and according to God's will. So the prophesy became open to the interpretation of "the Messiah", that is the interpretation of a king "anointed by the Lord" himself (Christos is the Greek translation of the word Messiah, i.e. anointed by God), an ideal king, not connected with dynasties, a king directly from God, a figure outside the usual power system, the bearer of a deep, lasting, inner freedom.

It is no chance that this is the text that begins the night of the Birth of the Lord in our Christian liturgy, reminding us that the promised child, the "eternal" king, the Prince of Peace is the little Jesus, long ago promised, the continuer of the history of salvation, the mediator between us and God, born to save us. The promise of life, of which he is the bearer, does not stop even before death: the pain and sorrow over the one "whom they pierced", as the prophet Zachariah reminds us, are the same as when "one mourneth for his only son, and shall be in bitterness for him as one that is in bitterness for his first-born".[14] That pain, that accompanies the child full of promise, the first-born, turns to joy, because death cannot hold him. The child Jesus is the sign of the resurrection, he is the victor over death and pain, as was prophesied by two further great prophets, Elijah and Elizeus, who returned two children to their mothers, their two only sons, who had died. This act of resurrection confirms that a child is not only a source of renewed hope and ceaseless joy and comfort, but it makes him an instrument through which we acknowledge the presence of the Lord himself, the presence of eternal life, resurrection, the definite victory over death. The words of the widow of Sarepta, which she spoke to Elijah after he had miraculously brought her child back to life: "Now by this I know that thou art a man of God and the word of the Lord in thy mouth is truth", are now comprehensible to him who recognises the child of Bethlehem' he who is the Word, the Word that was made flesh, the Word of God and eternal, that wants not to be a mere "sign" of future reality, of an ideal present, but the actual daily presence of salvation, incarnation, a sharing of the human fate, so that the Word of God should be seen and heard on the Earth in faith for all time.

3. THE CHILD JESUS

s we have already mentioned, the "gospels of childhood" as they are called (Matthew 1-2 and Luke 1-2) are the youngest of the gospels. When the story of the Life of Jesus had been written, the writer of the story, who had lived through it all, was most amazed by the mystery of the death and resurrection of the Lord Jesus. These stories, almost the same in all four gospels, are the beginning of the Christian Whitsun sermons[16], the basis of the gospels. Anyway, as a well-known theologian wrote some time ago, what can be said of someone when he comes into the world? A child is always the bearer of a certain promise, but it can never be said with certainty if it will be intelligent or not, if it will have a good heart or, on the contrary, become a scoundrel, if it will do something great and worth while and remain faithful to its choice to the end... All these questions remain unanswered till the end of that child's life, and every judgement must be postponed till the end of the earthly pilgrimage of every individual[17]. No one can be entirely sure of himself, because he who calls himself honest may slip, and an obvious sinner may turn and mend his ways, as is confirmed by biblical wisdom, based on events from very different times and places.

Around this core of the Easter mystery of the death and resurrection of Jesus Christ many stories have gradually accumulated of his preaching and parables, his brief and wise sayings, proverbs and observations that are easy to remember, also stories about miracles and the astounding effect of Jesus' words on those who listened to him with faith. Of course these facts were too momentous to be imparted as ordinary daily events. The invasion of the divine into the human did not this time occur through amazing natural phenomena, like an earthquake or thunder and lightning[18], but in the form of the humble and simple little figures of children that make their way through the whole Bible, as we have described.

The Evangelists, who composed these pages of the "gospels of childhood", wrote of the life of Jesus Christ on the basis of their own experience, they wrote of what they had seen with their own eyes, they had themselves listened to the first apostolic sermons. And when the old prophesies of Jewish wisdom are read through again, a new meaning is found in them, just as happens to us when we experience an event that we do not understand and then, if we look back, we find the key to it, the sense of all we have lived through. These pages originated when the preaching had exhausted all the essential themes, or when the first attacks of unbelievers forced a more exact formulation of some unclear passages of the Christian message[19]. What happened before Jesus was christened in the Jordan? Did Jesus come from Nazareth or from Bethlehem? If he was really the son of God, how could he be born like any other human being, in poverty and in hiding?

All these questions stand in the background of the story of the first chapters of the gospels of St. Matthew and St. Luke. They write down their stories in the spirit of what is known in Jewish circles under the name "midrash – search", which means search in the biblical texts, the search for connections and differences, or the explanation of one text in the light of another. Matthew's or Luke's "midrash" means searching for and explaining those elements that can help us better to draw a picture of the child that was born as the bearer of all promises, it is a child-God, a child that in its very name, Jesus, which means "God, help", contains within itself the promise of eternal salvation for everybody.

This "midrash" has linking historical, artistic and literary elements. The core of the events related by Matthew and Luke, although in quite different ways, because each of them starts from a different point of view and each speaks to a different audience, cannot be seriously discussed or doubted, despite the fact that some elements may seem pseudo-supernatural, like folklore etc. They are folk stories, related by knowledgeable authors not to knowledgeable people but to believers, to whom the author wants to give an important message. The sober and unostentatious style of the stories that makes no attempt at needless prolixity and does not waste words describing subsidiary things, testifies to the author's theological aim: the child that was born in Bethlehem, in Judaea, is the promised Messiah, he is the Saviour, who lives an eternal life, he is the beginning and the summit of all our longings and feelings, he is Jesus Christ, Our Lord.

4. APOCRYPHAL LITERATURE

At a certain period of our history, fifteen hundred years after the birth of that holy Child, it was considered necessary to distinguish between some books, that had always been highly valued by the Christian community, and others, also important, but not considered basic and decisive for our faith. The books that form our Bible today were divided from others, called the "apocrypha". This term was used even in ancient times to qualify books intended for a narrow, select circle of readers, but later it was used to qualify books that, though interesting in their way and popular with believers, were suspected of containing teachings that did not entirely correspond to the official teachings of the church, books that were excluded from being publicly read during liturgical ceremonies[20].

The apocrypha, books which have a certain importance owing to the interest in the Lord's childhood, were books that, evidently or tacitly, wanted to be recognised as equally valid with the books of the bible. They dealt with the same themes and wanted to replace or complement the books of the Bible known as the "canon". They do not, of course, interest us for this reason, as the books of the Bible, for their sober and basic character, need no completion, they contain everything to nourish our belief[21]. But the books of the apocrypha are an important and ancient proof that there existed in the Christian communities of the first centuries various forms of teaching and various interests. These books penetrate much more into detail, trying to expose something sensational, they contain fantastic, novel-like stories, opening up a wide field of curiosity. They are an expression of the strong religious feeling of the people in the first centuries after Christ.

What interests us in these writings are just the parts that deal with Jesus' childhood. The questions behind these texts are the same as those we drew attention to in the "canon" stories about the childhood in the gospels of St. Matthew and St. Luke. What was the true origin of Jesus and his family? How can we explain his being born to a virgin? Who were Mary's parents? Not many people know that the liturgical commemoration of the namedays of Mary's parents, Joachim and Anna, whom we now celebrate as saints, originates only from these books, without which we should not even know their names. The same is true of the festival of the Presentation of Mary in the Temple, which is written of in the text called "The Protevangel of James", or also "On the Birth of Mary". And what should be said of the ox and the ass, that are always pictured around the little Jesus in works of art? Or the fact that the kings who came from the East to visit Jesus in the manger were said to be three, and that their names were Caspar, Melichar and Balthazar?

These are only a few examples of the influence these books have had on our popular tradition, especially in art, from Palestine to Byzantium, from the time of the Roman catacombs to Renaissance days. From these books we learn of the piety of the first generation of Christians, of their failings and their character, longings and interests and of religious customs of which we are still to a great extent the heritors. As an example of their character and extent, we may name just some of the most important texts: "On the Birth of the Virgin Mary" (Protoevangelium Jacobi), "Pseudo-Evangelium Matthaei"[22], The Gospel of St. Thomas, also known amongst the Malabar Indians, and the so-called "Arabian Gospel on the Saviour's Childhood" – this is a text from the 5th century that had an important influence on the writing of the Koran.

On the basis of examination of this Christian literature of the first centuries one can trace the devotion that people feel towards Jesus' childhood, a devotion that continues to us, the generation of the present and to the Prague Child Jesus. A multitude of voices glorify God the Child, the eyes of the crowd admire him in ecstasy and extol the coalescence of the human and the divine. The Child Jesus tells us of God's plans, of the divine mystery itself. We admire in him the love of the Father who, through the power of the Holy Ghost, makes himself visible in human form in the womb of a young Jewish woman and allows his words to be audible to us again in human form. But there is something more here. He speaks to us of our secrets, he tells man about man – it is the divine mission inscribed in the human one. The little Jesus, delicate and poor, unknown and in flight, rejected and laid in the stable where the animals were wont to go for their food, is at the same time a Child encompassed with fame and heavenly hosts that sing his praises. He is the Child for whom the wise men set out on a long journey, bringing him gifts. He is the Child for whom other innocent children give their lives, auguring his deed of sacrificing his own life, and this sacrifice is made by many martyrs, who are willing to make it for his love.

He is a child and the King of Heaven, a suckling and at the same time He who provides true nourishment. He is born in the dark of night and is at the same time He who is foretold by the light of a great star, He who gives light unto all nations. He is a real Jew who brings to fulfilment the mission of his people – to acquaint all nations with the name of the true and only God. And while he abolishes all racial privileges and breaks down the dividing walls between nations, all those who believe in him will consider themselves as brothers – each other's brothers and the brothers of Jesus, as sons in the Son of the same Father. For him God will be praised and he will himself be the object of prayers and of praise: "And Mary said: I saw glorifying angels around us, who fell at the feet of my son and sang, saying – Blessed be thy name, O God, that thou hast come into this wretchedness to save Adam and his sons, whom thou hast created with thine own hands. Blessed be the first Word that came from the mouth of the Father, Lord of all, and glory to thy Mother, the Holy Virgin, who suffered with thee in thy holy birth".[23]

p Marco Chiolerio ocd

1 Proverbs 22.15, 23.13

2 Genesis 4.25

3 Genesis 11.30

4 Genesis 25.21

5 Genesis 29.31, 30.22

6 Judges 13. 2-3

7 1 Samuel 1.5-20

8 Luke 1.7, 36

9 1 Samuel 2.5, Psalm 113.9

10 2 Samuel 12. 14-18

11 Numbers 11.12

12 Jeremiah 31.20

13 Isaiah 7.3 etc.

14 Zachariah 12.10

15 1 Kings 17.17-24 and 2 Kings 4.8-37

16 Acts 2.14-41, 4.23-31, 1 Kings 2.2

17 C. MOLARI, Si fece uomo. Christmas Meditation (Rome 1982) 30

18 Exodus 19, Psalm 18 and many other texts

19 ORTENSIO DA SPINETOLI, Introduzione ai vangeli dell Infanzia (Brescia 1967) 12.

20 The "canon" is spoken of as a rule or norm in Galatians 15-16 and 2 Kings 10.13-16. For the term "apocrypha" see IRENAEUS, Adv. Haer. I, 20.1 TERTULLIANUS, De pud. 10,12.

21 IRENAEUS, Adv. Haer III, 1: "He who shall scorn the teaching of the Apostles, scorns the Lord himself". ORIGENES, In Lc. hom. praefatio, compares those who tried to surpass the apostles by writing "their" gospels, to the false prophets of the Old Testament, see EUSEBIUS OF CAESAREA, Hist. Eccl. 3.25. AUGUSTINUS, De doctr. christ. 2.8.

22 The frescos in the ancient Roman temple "Fortuna virilis", rebuilt into a Christian church, dated 872-882, are based on this pseudo-gospel from the 4th century probably, which was known to Hieronymus and Augustin.

23 L. MORALDI, Apocrifi del Nuovo Testamento (Turin 1971) I. 46.

A YEAR

I.
January

Snowy soft light
kisses the fleeting snowflakes

The universe is pure white
it is new-born

So can a Christian be born
anew
like a pure white snowflake of this moment

And begin
begin again
washed by the light

Oh Prague Child Jesus
grant us the strength
to be born again

II.
February

Freezing darkness
crushes the Earth

Oh Prague Child Jesus
grant
that we may not forget:

Winter
is the name of Spring
that is coming

III.
March

Barefoot children
staggering
through the storm

The storm of poverty
clouts
anxiety

Oh Prague Child Jesus
grant
that I may see you
in every child
in the whole world

In every child
who is at this moment crying

IV.
April

Daybreak
From the blessing hand
of the Prague Child Jesus
ceaselessly
the rays take wing and soar

At the same time
an angel sings:

Catch a single ray
And you will live

Catch a single ray
and you will not fear
the dark

V.
May

Spring gives
the bread of light

The Child of Spring
on the Prague altar
is smiling

Dear child
give with your eyes
the bread of light
and with your heart
the bread of love

VI.
June

The gentle hand of light
stroking the horizon

Oh Prague Child Jesus
may we have the strength
to be a home
to our dear ones

May every word
that we utter
be a door
to our hearts

A joyously wide open door

VII.
July

The landscape is flickering
silently glowing

Oh Prague Child Jesus
may we too be silent
like all
veritable
victors

Every victory
has the name
of patience

VIII.
August

A crystal breath
floats down from the blazing sky

Oh Prague Child Jesus
grant
that we may breathe
the breath of the saints

Holiness
signifies
to lay each day
on the altar

Including today

IX.
September

Time has ripened
Its harvest time

The beginning
of the harvest of hope

Oh Prague Child Jesus
may we have ever
full granaries
of hope
full granaries
of longings

X.
October

A thousand colours
have blossomed

A thousand colours
have flooded the universe

Oh Prague Child Jesus
grant
that for the colours
we do not forget
the painter

XI.
November

From the lighted graves
comes song:
We shall meet again
From the lighted graves
comes song:
We love you

From the lighted graves
comes song:
Love each other

Oh Prague Child Jesus
grant
that we do not fail to hear
the voice of the lighted graves

XII.
December

A pure white silence
falls upon the landscape

And in the darkness
a window shines

At the end of every darkness
a window shines

The window of Bethlehem

Oh Prague Child Jesus
grant
that at the end of every darkness
we may see
the light of Bethlehem